AN EASY-READ COMMUNITY BOOK

WHERE DO YOU GO TO SCHOOL?

BY CAROLINE ARNOLD

PHOTOGRAPHS BY CAROLE BERTOL

Franklin Watts
New York/London/Toronto/Sydney
1982

Special thanks are due the following individuals and organizations whose cooperation made the photographs possible:

Apex Technical School; Kathryn Hilt; Kathleen Hopkins; The Irwin S. Chanin School of Architecture of the Cooper Union; Jack Nacmias; Wm. A. Reeves; Stonewall Jackson Junior High School.

Photographs courtesy of: page 10, Sam Falk; page 11, Pro Pix; page 13, Freda Leinwand; page 23, Mimi Forsyth, all from Monkmeyer Press Photo Service

R.L. 2.6 Spache Revised Formula

Library of Congress Cataloging in Publication Data

Arnold, Caroline.
Where do you go to school?

(An Easy-read community book)
Includes index.
Summary: Briefly discusses types of schools, the variety of jobs performed by people who work in them, and what people do at school.
1. Schools—United States—Juvenile literature.
[1. Schools] I. Bertol, Carole, ill. II. Title.
III. Series.
LA210.A78   1982   371   82-8647
ISBN 0-531-04442-4   AACR2

Text copyright © 1982 by Caroline Arnold
Illustrations copyright © 1982 by Franklin Watts, Inc.
All rights reserved
Printed in the United States of America
6 5 4 3 2 1

CONTENTS

Your School	5
Who Works at Your School?	14
What Do You Do at School?	24
Who Goes to School?	31

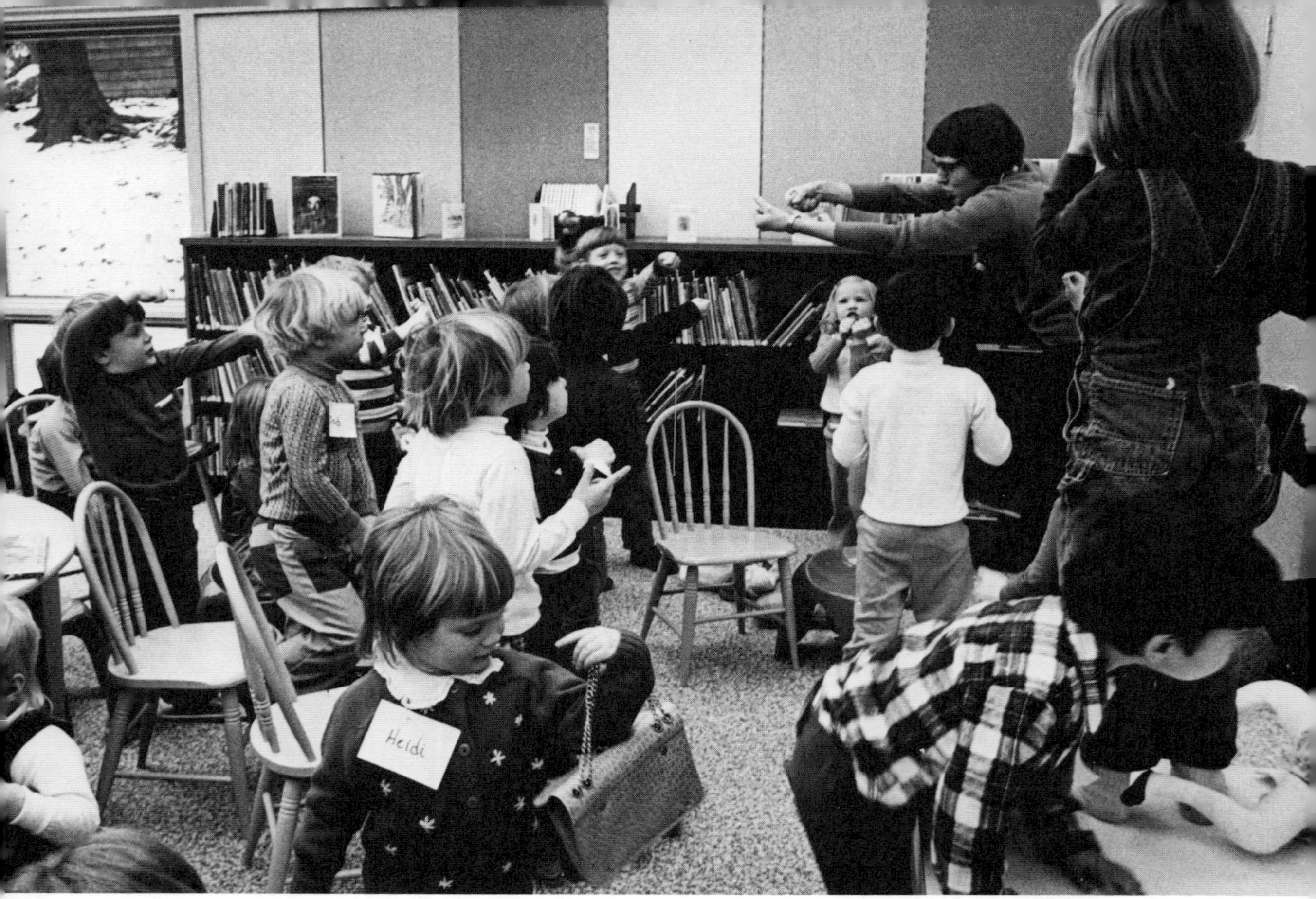
Heidi

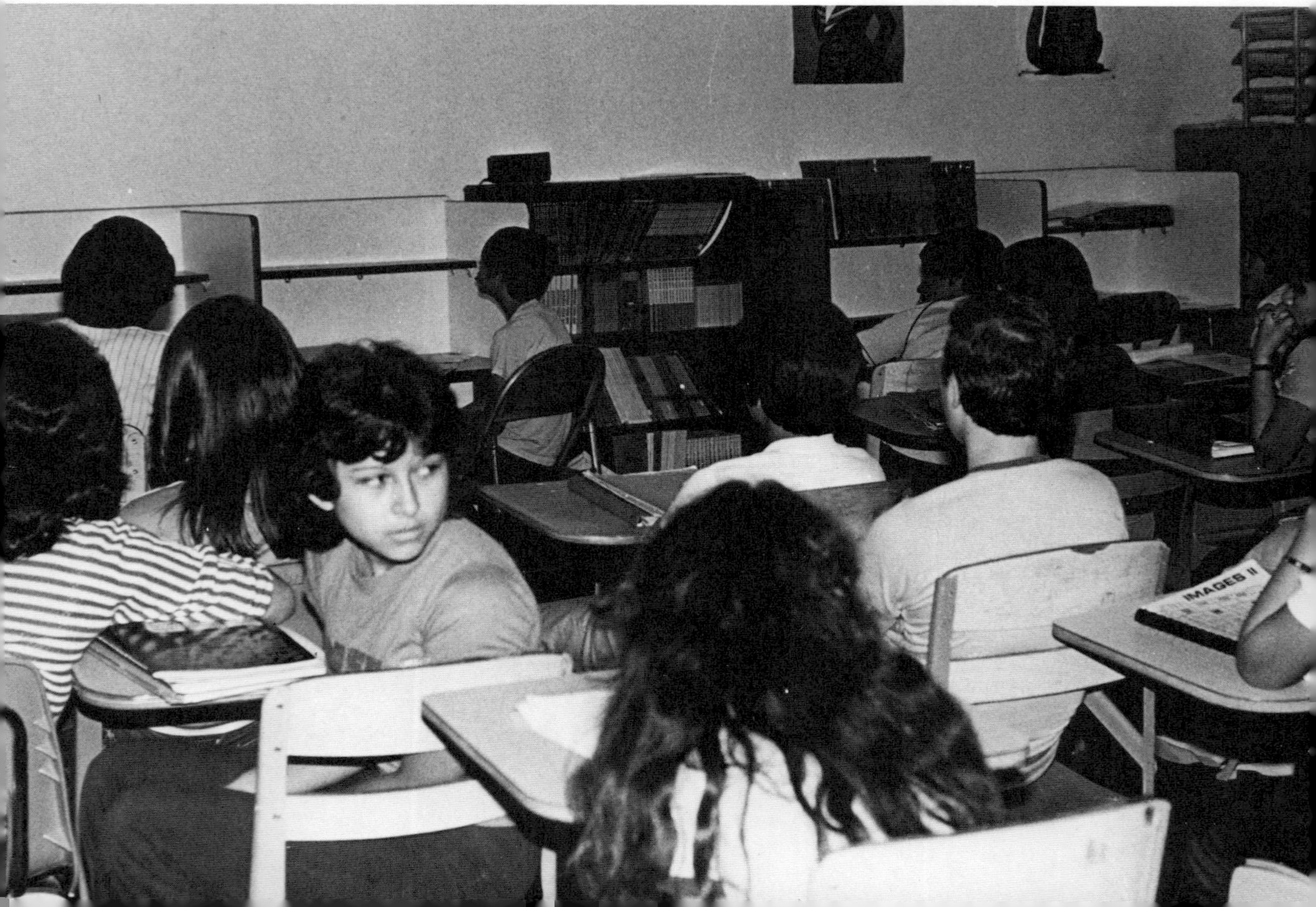
IMAGES II

Your School

There are many kinds of schools in the community. Some are big and some are small. Some are for children. Some are for adults. Some are public and some are private.

What kind of school do you go to?

Nursery schools are for children too young to go to kindergarten. Not all children go to nursery schools.

Most children start kindergarten when they are five. Elementary schools are usually for children from kindergarten to sixth grade.

Junior high schools are usually for children in grades seven, eight, and nine. High school is usually for grades ten, eleven, and twelve.

Most people finish high school. After that some people get jobs. Some go to college or other schools. They may go to school to learn how to be a nurse, to work computers, or to fix cars. They may learn how to be a doctor, a lawyer, or an engineer. What you learn in school helps you to get a job.

Where is your school? Is it in your neighborhood? It may be so close that you can walk there by yourself.

You must be careful when you cross busy streets. You must obey the crossing guard if there is one.

Sometimes your school is far away from where you live. Then you must ride in a car or bus.

The bus may pick you up at your house. Or you may wait at a bus stop. When the bus comes you get on. Then you ride to school.

A long time ago children who lived in the country went to small schools near their homes. There were just one or two teachers in the school. Each class had children in many grades.

Today there are still a few schools like that. But most children who live in the country go to school in a nearby town. Sometimes a few towns join together and build one big school.

Everyone must learn to read and write and work with numbers. Our government provides schools and teachers so people can learn. These are public schools. They are free and open to all.

Some people prefer other kinds of schools. These are called private schools. People must pay to go to private schools.

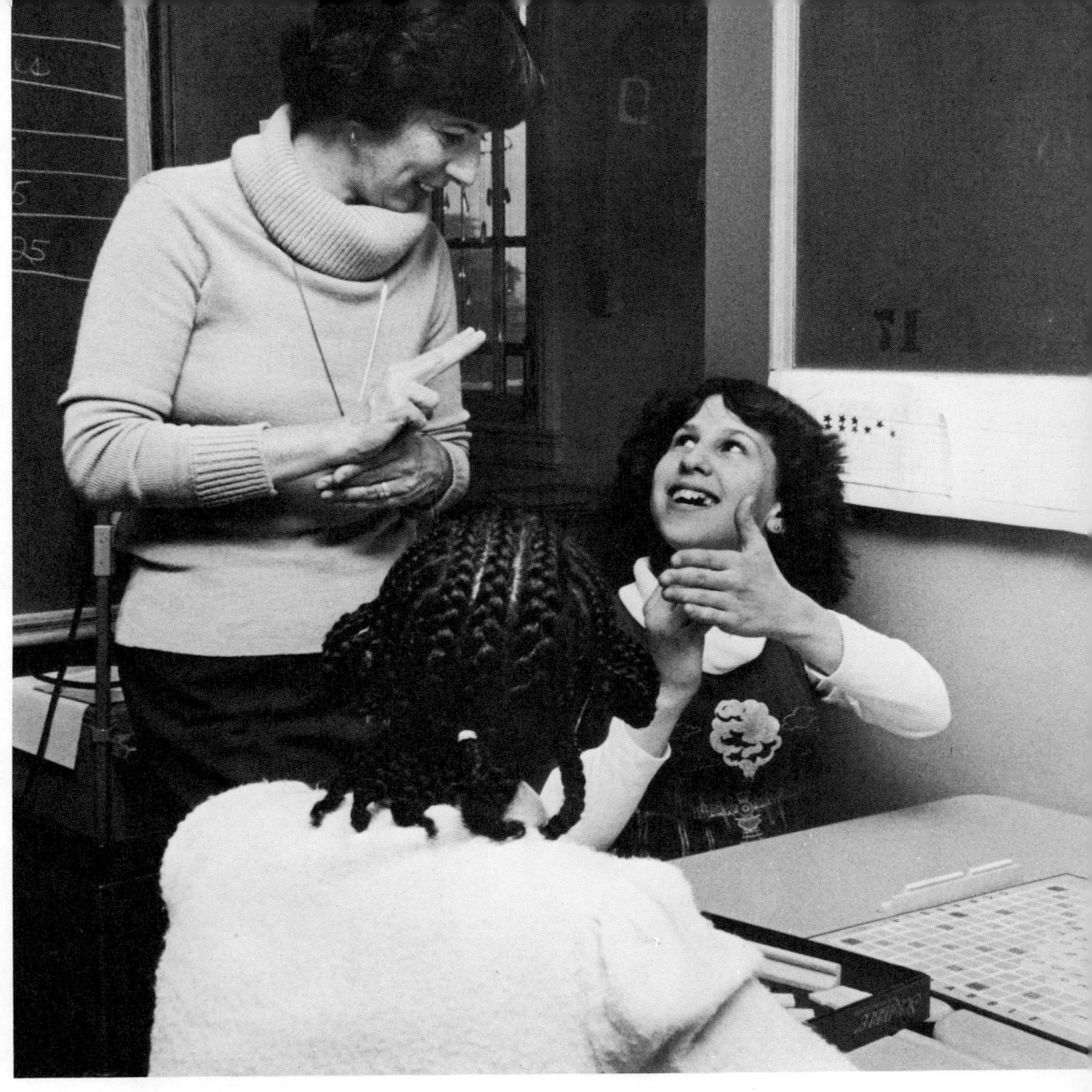

Some children need special schools. There are schools for blind children and for deaf children. There are schools for children with learning problems and for children in wheelchairs.

Who Works at Your School?

Many people work at schools.

Each classroom has a teacher. He or she helps the children learn. An aide may help, too. Sometimes parents help in the classroom.

Sometimes your teacher gets sick. He or she cannot come to school. Then you will have a substitute teacher. The substitute will help you learn until your teacher comes back.

You may have teachers in your school who teach just one thing.

A music teacher teaches you how to sing, how to play an instrument, and how to listen to music.

An art teacher teaches you how to draw and paint, how to build shapes, and how to make crafts.

A speech teacher helps children to speak clearly.

A special reading teacher helps some children to read.

We all need exercise. We need to learn how to do things with our bodies. A physical education teacher teaches games, sports, fitness, gymnastics, and dancing.

You may do some of these things with your classroom teacher, too.

In your classroom there are many books. But sometimes you cannot find the book you need. Then you can go to the library.

The librarian will help you to find a book.

If your school does not have a librarian, your teacher or a helper may show you how to find books.

The principal of your school works in an office. He or she meets with students, teachers, and other school workers. The principal sees that everything in the school runs smoothly.

In the school office there are people who answer the telephones, type, and keep attendance records.

The custodian helps to keep the school clean and in good repair.

Do you eat lunch at school? Some children eat breakfast at school, too.

Many schools have a cafeteria. People there cook food and serve it to the children.

Some children bring their lunch to school in a bag or lunchbox.

Many schools have a school nurse.
Sometimes you do not feel well at school. Then you can go to the nurse's office. The nurse will take care of you until you go home or until you feel better.

The nurse can also bandage cuts and scrapes if you get hurt.

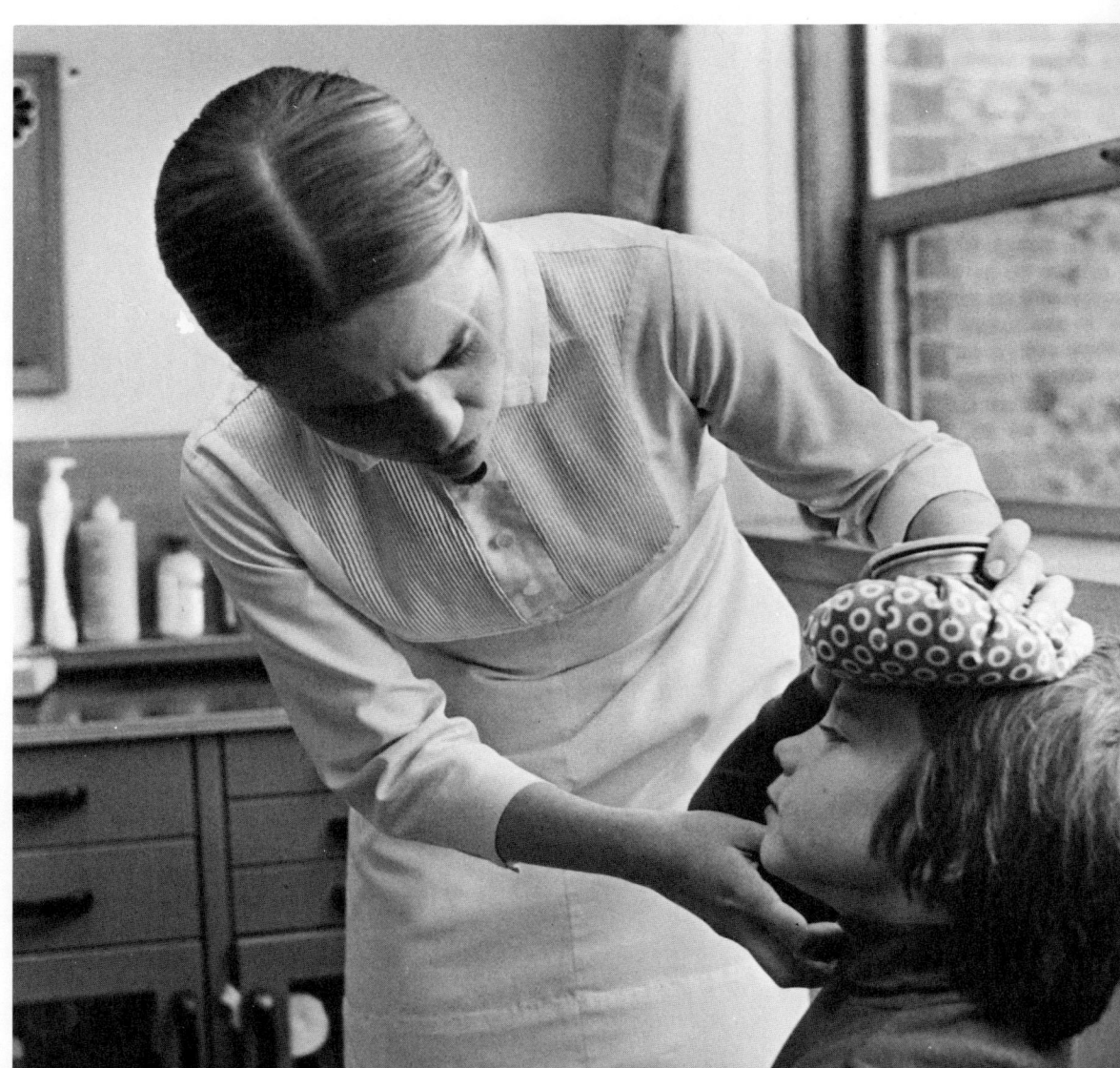

What Do You Do at School?

You learn many things at school. You learn to listen, to follow directions, and how to get along with others.

In reading you learn to read and write words.

In math you learn to work with numbers.

In social studies you learn about the world we live in.

In science you learn about plants and animals, about the earth and the universe, and about how our bodies work.

In physical education you learn how to do things with your body.

When you finish the
To be good readers, we must learn to make judgements based on the information found in what we read.

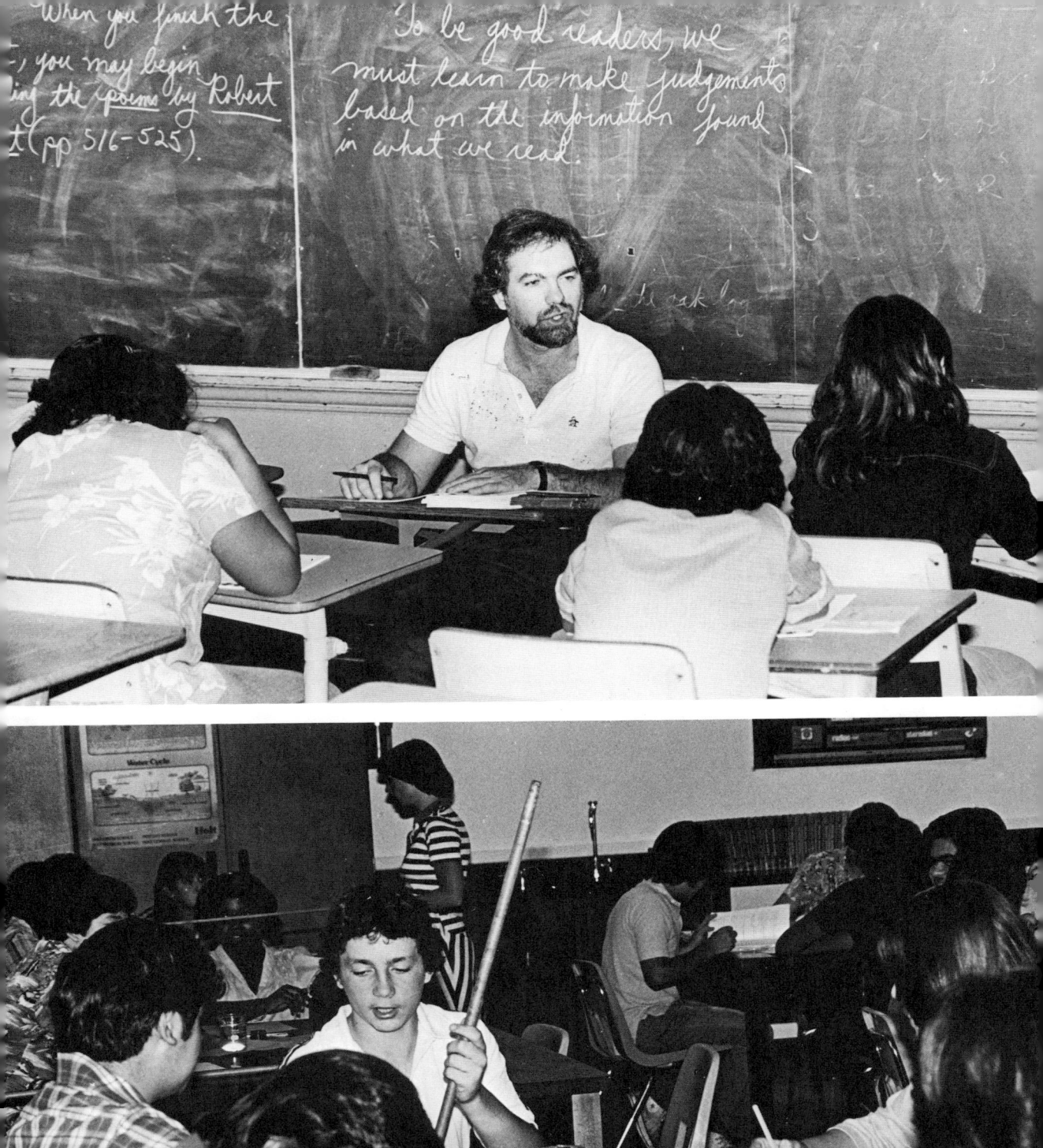

People learn in many ways.
They learn by listening to the teacher,
by writing on paper or in a workbook,
by reading and by looking at pictures,
by playing games,
by watching films or television,
by doing experiments,
by talking with each other,
and by going on trips.

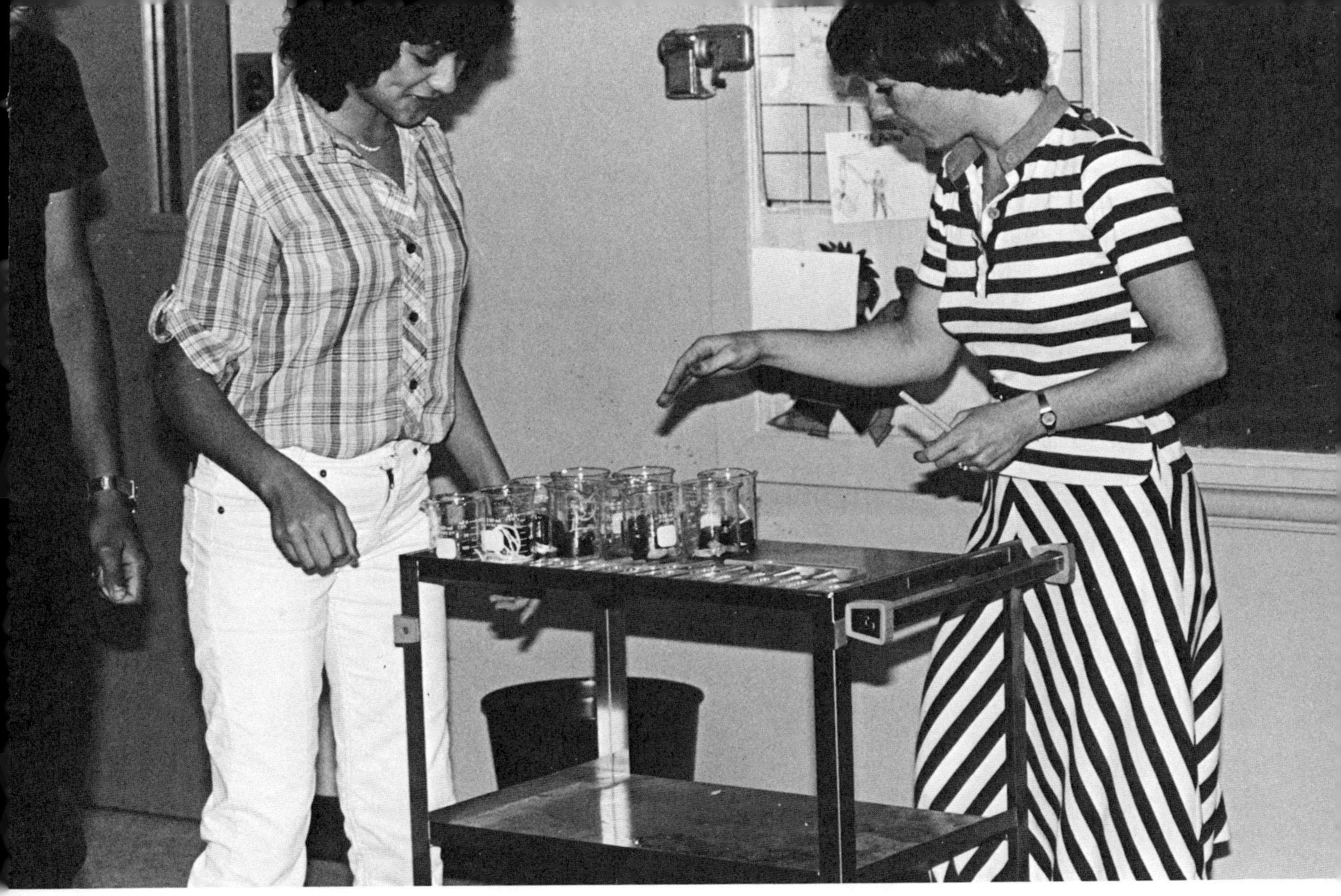

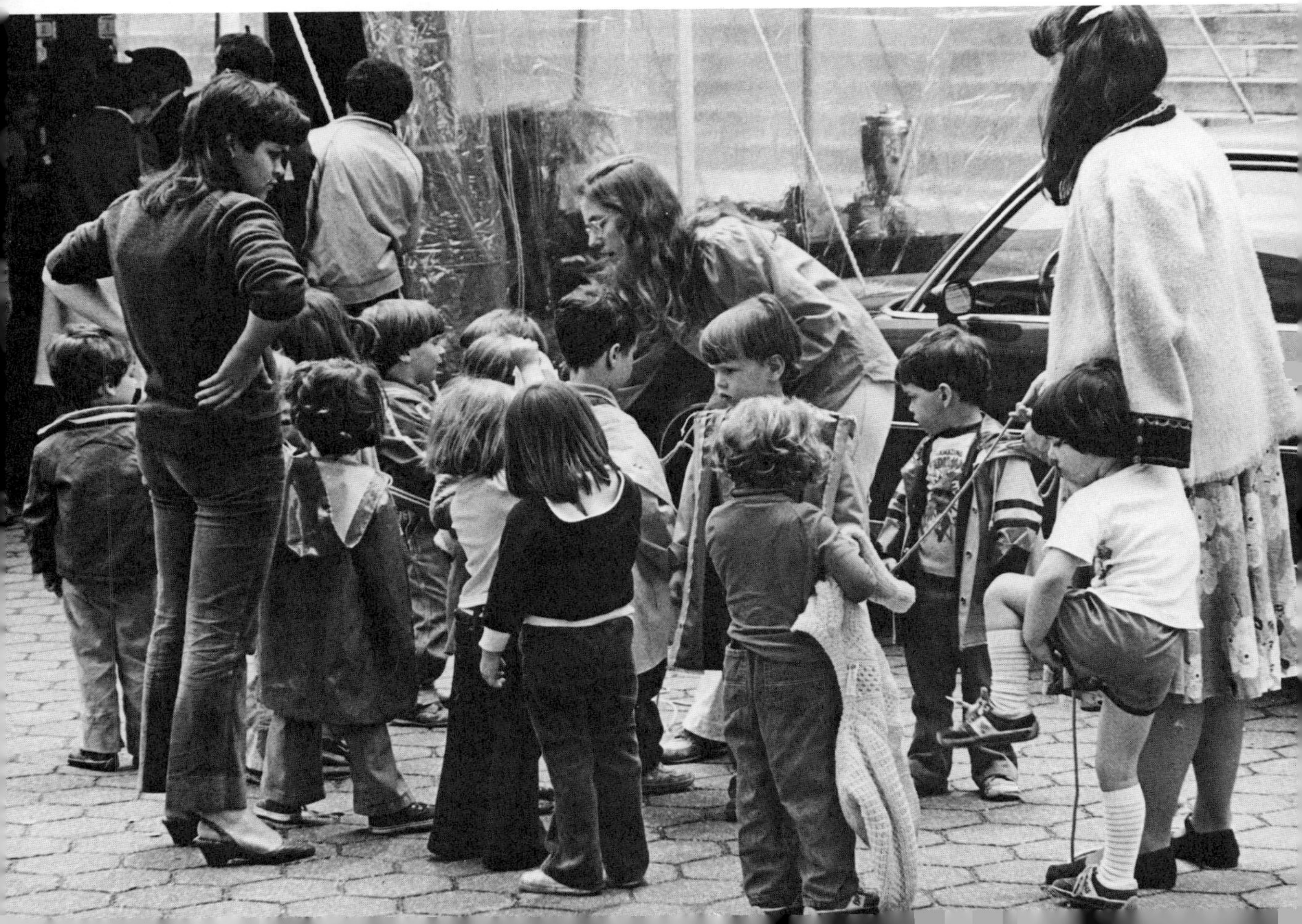

It is hard to sit still and work all day. Recess is a good time to run and play.

At the end of the school day it is time to go home. Sometimes you may have homework.

After school some children take special classes. They may take music, gymnastic, or dancing lessons. They may also play a sport on a neighborhood team.

Who Goes to School?

Sometimes learning is hard work. But learning can be fun, too.

No one is too old to learn.

Sometimes adults want to learn something they did not learn when they went to school. Then they may take classes at a nearby high school or college. Or they may take classes at a community center.

Schools teach us things we need to know. They also bring people together in the community.